You Will Feel It
in the
Price of Bread

You Will Feel It in the Price of Bread

Katya Hudson

MUSWELL
PRESS

First published by Muswell Press in 2023
Copyright © Katya Hudson 2023

Typeset by e-Digital Design
Printed and bound by CPI (UK) Ltd, Croydon CR0 4YY

ISBN: 9781739193041
eISBN: 9781739193058

A CIP catalogue record for this book is available from the British Library

Muswell Press
London N6 5HQ
www.muswell-press.co.uk

Newspaper front pages reproduced with permission:
dmg media licensing
Mirrorpix
News Corp UK

Newspaper images reproduced with permission:
The Times / News Licensing
Reach Licensing / Mirrorpix
dmg media licensing

A royalty from the sale of this book will be donated to the Ukraine
Humanitarian Appeal www.dec.org.uk

I dedicate this book to my 'rodyna' now spread far and wide.

To my mother, who travels back to Ukraine too often for me to react anymore.

    To my father, who keeps saying 'how lucky we are, considering'.

    To my sister who continues to do clothes sales to fund the Ukrainian army.

    To my brother who sends me Ukrainian army memes.

    And of course, to Babushka with whom a year on, I am finally reunited.

    Who yesterday mistook the sound of a vacuum cleaner for sirens.

    Who tries her hardest to only speak Ukrainian now.

    Who, sitting across from me now as I write, wears a t-shirt on which 'HOPE' is printed in silver English letters. I don't think she knows what it says.

I dedicate this book to the people of Ukraine, my home, my 'rodyna'.

Childhood

I was born on 21st January in Kyiv, Ukraine. On what she describes as a bitterly cold day, Mama gave birth to me in a state hospital that has existed since the USSR. My dad wasn't allowed in the room. I was small: when she held me on her arm, with my head in her hand, my toes didn't reach her elbow. She named me Katya, Katherine for my English dad.

In the office, from left to right: Lada (Mama), Beatty (my sister), me, Tetya Zhana (my aunt).

I spoke Russian at home, Ukrainian at school, English to my dad. Watching TV on a pirated Sky box, we would get English programmes, then later we had the luxury of Disney and Cartoon Network. My parents were always at work; my dad was an architect and Mama a linguist. Together they ran a real estate company, usually coming home at nine at night. When I heard their keys in the door I would jump out of bed and run down our long yellow corridor to hug the cold of their coats.

In the morning my Dad would make coffee for my mum, hot chocolate for me and Beatty (my younger sister), with his special 'frothy' technique. Then he would make us packed lunches, sandwiches usually on brown bread, usually soggy by the time we ate them at school from the pickles between the cheese.

After school, my Babushka (grandmother) would pick us up. She busied herself making stacks of pancakes, which we would eat with jam from the Dacha. A Dacha is a small plot of land, a summer house outside of the city used to relax and cultivate fruit and vegetables; common for Ukrainian families.

Our Dacha was in Poltava. Bought by Zhana and her late husband Serozha as far from the Chernobyl disaster as possible. It was a place to get away from city life and breathe clean air. In childhood, this place was full of family, berries and washing ourselves in the shower outside, its water heated in a vat by the sun. We would brave the outdoor toilet, a glorified pit in the ground, where the spiders were sustained by my cousin Yaroslav, who caught and fed them flies. On the long road to the river, we'd steal handfuls of berries from branches overhanging fences. This walk was soundtracked by the recounting of my grandmother's latest book.

Babushka Zhana

If I could only pick one, Babushka Zhana is my favourite person on earth. She raised me. She's funny, I think she's in her 80s. 'I've told so many people different things I can't remember which lie to keep up', she tells me; I can't tell if she's joking. A paediatrician, a grandmother to five, a great grandmother to two, a strong swimmer, ruthless at cards and an inveterate consumer of steamy romantic novels. I am the only grandchild that gets the privilege of hearing the really saucy stuff, she tells me, thrilled. She also fancies most men under the age of forty, pointing out who she has the hots for as we sit on the metro. 'There was no sex in the USSR', she tells me with a wicked smile.

She buys my friends woolly socks when they visit, she makes huge vats of borsch, high stacks of pancakes and vareniki (pillowy dumplings) in summer, stuffed with frozen sour cherries collected at the Dacha the summer before. She doesn't like being still, she likes being useful. Almost a foot taller than her now, I still get out of breath running after her.

Babushka remembers World War Two when her mother was taken by the Germans. She hated them until much later in life she tells me, biased by memories of

Babushka (on the left hugged by son in law – my dad) at her 80th birthday with daughters, grandchildren and great-grandchildren.

past atrocities. She thought all Germans were evil, until we had a neighbour move in upstairs. Their child fell ill, and a conflicted Babushka came to help. Through healing the German child, she realised it was not nationality that made monsters. She only really talks about her past when I beg her and she can be persuaded to take a breath from the latest romance. Much more interesting is her life.

Zhana, Kyiv in the summer.

Zhana and Volodia (top right) on hiking holiday in Crimea.

Zhana and Volodia with their second daughter Lada (Mama).

Before, when Babushka was just Zhana, I think she spoke Russian in her family, and was often looked after by what she calls the 'babenki', old women of some standing who spoke Ukrainian and French. When her mother was taken by the Germans to a work camp, Babushka was taken in by a Jewish doctor who often treated the sickly child. A kind man, whose religion was kept secret by his village neighbours. His wife wasn't opposed to giving Babushka a good beating.

Babushka was inspired by the doctor and decided to follow the same profession. She moved to Kyiv for university and never left. There she met my grandfather on a victory day march. Volodia was a strong, stubborn, and at times, harsh figure. Volodia deemed gynaecology an embarrassing specialism for his future wife, so Zhana became a paediatrician.

Volodia grew up in a partisan village. His father's location was secret, I've heard tales of his mother being forced to watch as the Germans threw Volodia against a wall in a bid to reveal his father's location. He recalled narrowly avoiding being shot by Germans soldiers in the woods. Volodia would walk for hours to school and back each day. A force to be reckoned with, an engineer specialising in welding of rockets, so presumably missiles.

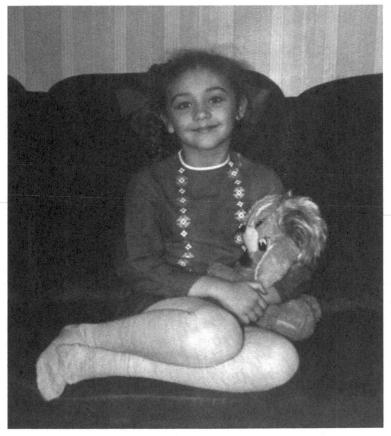

Lada.

I remember him later in life: to me he was Dedushka, the grandfather who would buy me bitter dark chocolate with hazelnut. Working as a security guard at my parent's office at night, he would cook his speciality regularly, microwaving pears and brewing strong black tea. At Christmas he would consistently beat my dad at chess.

Stubborn, he once drank a whole litre of honey for a dare, and his circulation never recovered: meaning he struggled with inflated legs and running sores. He never once left what was the USSR, repeatedly and proudly rejecting offers of holidays to Turkey in favour of going to Crimea.

For fear of dirt, newspapers covered the floor in their USSR flat, where Volodia and Zhana lived with their two daughters: small Zhana (Mama's older sister) and Lada (Mama). Later they were joined first by little Zhana's husband, and then two boys. Seven people in two bedrooms. Two engineers, two doctors, a linguist and two children, this was the poor equality of the Soviet Union.

Lada with neighbour boy.

Mama often tells of her first taste of a Mars bar. A luxury her father bought once, which he sliced into seven pieces to be shared by the family.

My grandmother remembers the bread queues of the USSR; my memories of bread are different...

Bread

I remember Pampushki. Small, doughy, perfectly rounded bread buns, with small garlic chips stuck to their shiny tops. At the Dacha we hear the bread truck ringing out its presence. In hot summer, it is heard outside while working in the field at the Dacha. My sister and I run ahead on Babushka's command, we don't want to miss it! We queue up at the big blue truck, peering in at its wealth of bread piled high. The van would drive off on the flat road, disappearing behind golden wheat fields, sunflowers growing high; we dip our freshly baked bread into hot red borsch made from vegetables freshly dug, topped with a dollop of sour cream.

Lunch at the Dacha.

I remember the chewy factory-baked white loaf they slather with butter at school, rubbery, we each get a slice. I remember my boyfriend at eight, gifts me his. How lucky I am, I put it into my bag eagerly for later, only for it to be found by my grandmother, melted over maths homework.

Pampushki.

Brown brick rye bread.

Crimean flat bread.

'Freedom Bread'.

I remember Crimean summers; on the train carriage back home we share fresh flatbread, torn with hot, sandy and sun-tanned hands. Whole cucumbers, large tomatoes bitten like apples, sweet from Chernozer, our fertile and famed black earth, with hot black tea with lemon and sugar cubes. My grandad lets me have the flower moulded in the dough at the centre, petals I would eat one by one. He loves me, he loves me not, under my breath, the centre saved for last.

We would go once a year to a Crimean sanatorium, a remnant of the USSR. The beach was pebbly and the sea warm, women would run up and down vending berries in plastic cups topped with sugar. The sea was good for my grandfather's legs. Somewhere on that beach in Almaz still lies my last baby tooth. Bitten into a hot corn on the cob sold on that beach. I wondered why there was ketchup on my cob.

School project, title reads: 'My holiday and geography'. A map of Ukraine with Crimea coloured in.

Kyiv wasn't cool yet

Turning thirteen, I discovered YouTube, *Wild Child* and Avril Lavigne. Ukraine wasn't cool anymore. Western culture called – it sounded like One Direction. Here came the obsession with Union Jacks and the strong desire to go to boarding school. Oh, the first years of freedom from parents, Primark and any sugar I could buy from the daily tuck shop.

One winter, coming to Kyiv was different. Ukraine was dark. For reasons I didn't particularly understand at the time, Ukrainians were in revolution, Euromaidan had begun.

After months of hope and a western future Ukrainian President Yanukovich chose closer links with Russia and more government corruption. Yanukovich was rumoured to be paid by Putin. This sparked a nationwide revolution, its central hotspot in Kyiv on Maidan, the main square. Maidan started as a peaceful protest but turned violent when in December Berkrut forces got involved to clear the peaceful dissidents. A reported million citizens came out on the main street of Kreschatik and Maidan Nezaleznosti (Independence Square), to protest and remove Yanukovich.

During the day we would walk around the military-style tents, barracks of a sort, with the steaming vats of communal soup mixed with the scent of burning tires. At night we would hear snipers' gunshots. This year the big Christmas tree placed in the centre was decorated with protest flags.

I think this was the first time I was proud of being Ukrainian. There was an energy. In the headlines, on the TV, Ukraine prevailed and was starting to be seen no longer as 'some place next to Russia'. The people were unified, they were Ukrainian.

The tension between Ukraine and Putin had been building for some time but this was a great stride, marked not only by fire and bullets but a revolution in the type of life Ukrainians wanted to live – proud, free and European.

Hearing changes

The Ukrainian language has long been a target, first of the Russian Empire, then the USSR and now Putin's oxymoronic sovereign democracy. All with the same aim: an attempt to steal our voice, our culture, our freedom. As a result, one language was spoken on formal occasions and another at home but recently the roles have switched: before Russian was the formal form but no longer, now Ukrainian is. The steps of making it the formal language, now spoken in schools, has meant that it is spoken among the young, between friends, trickling into families that were previously Russian speaking.

Ten years after leaving, I returned to Kyiv and moved back in with my family. I noticed not only the clothes but the words in Ukraine changed. Aside from the volatile events in 2013/14, there has been a decided cultural shift which can be heard in Ukraine. Ukrainian is spoken by the young in the fashionable coffee shops, restaurants and clubs, examples of small businesses taking up and developing western ideas. Replacing their affiliations with Russia with their new aspiring western style of life. No longer a cog in Putin's political machine, gone was the cigar smoke and cheap champagne, gift-wrapped by corrupt 'beeznessmeni' of the east. Speaking Russian carried a legacy of violence, false promises and brainwashing in bullshit.

Covid forced me back to Kyiv and I hoped it would not be for long, I worried about missing London – the art scene, the culture, the fashion. But now Kyiv felt different

Birch trees in the woods by Alice's house.

from the backwards place I had left. This new yet familiar place wore new clothes, was fuelled by readily available coffee, drunk by young artists, entrepreneurs and designers in European cafe society. My only friend still left from school was Alice. Like me, Alice left Ukraine at thirteen, coming back in 2020 to be with her family who live on the outskirts of Kyiv in a house in the woods.

Drawing of Alice.

She carries only cash, her house is decorated in designer furniture and her clothes carry expensive labels, from a time in the past when the family was better off, before certain dubious business and governmental connections were excised. Together, we rediscovered the city of our childhood. Frequenting the new vintage shops for clothes, restaurants for lunch and fashionable bars for cocktails, it was an intoxicating mix of low cost and luxury, in comparison to my life in London and Alice's in New York at least.

It was at one of these bars where we met Sasha and Nikita, whose grasp of the English language came primarily from TV's *Sex and the City* quotes. We formed a language of our own Russian, spiked with English pop culture. We met in Kashtan for coffee, drank purple cocktails in TCP bar and ate oreshki, shortbread biscuits in the shape of two walnut halves stuck together with condensed milk. Nikita and Sasha were newcomers to Kyiv and coming from Crimea they had seen first-hand the Russification that had taken place there since Putin's invasion in 2014; an attempted resurrection of the USSR. They saw themselves as Ukrainian.

A love letter, forget French, whisper Ukrainian in my ear. After a year of living in Kyiv, it had my heart, my soul my spirit.

After a year in the city, I found myself on my way to the Dacha. Three hours from Kyiv Central in the shaky elektrichka (train carriage) which smells of wee. As men stand smoking out of the windows, their cigarette smoke wafts from the door and women wade through carriages selling hot pirozhki (buns) stuffed with meat, potato, cabbage or cherry; out of a plastic bag insulated with tea towels. Where Babushkas and Tetyas (aunties) fight over seats with their plastic sacks tied to trolleys filled to overflowing with veg from the Dacha. You can hear Surzhyk, a mix of Russian and Ukrainian, and spoken, I suppose, as a residue of Russian colonialism. Mocked by most, Mama pointed out the beauty in it. An audible fracture in the system.

Dacha

That summer I experienced the Dacha without the rose tint of childhood memory. Time in the selo (village) is hard, long and mind-clearing. When working the land, breaking the large clumps out of soil becomes your main concern. Your list of tasks grows with the doing of the previous, time moves on, the changing seasons are visible in the soft black earth.

There is never nothing to do. Get wet, get hot, rise at dawn. The soil is still there, the vegetables ready themselves.

All work here is self-motivated, without any goal except that of doing. You don't need to grow veg, you can buy it for cheap. But the rain hasn't stopped, why should you? Stop? On the list of jobs not written down. A list of toils is made by seeing what needs to be done. Jobs never finished. Changing like the land around, seasonal, familiar, expected. Isolated in the land, a further distance from your neighbours than in the city, you are closer in spirit, in your dependence on others.

Miroslava brings my grandmother her milk, her cow grazes on the grass outside our gate. The pump to the well is broken, until fixed we depend on Miroslava's grandson, hoisting three-litre bottles from their well over the fence.

The Dacha kitchen.

From the field on the left, a man I don't know walks toward us and smiles at my Babushka. The neighbour offers beans of the non-magical variety. Eaten fresh or frozen for soup he tells us their properties. His visit is not solely for the purpose of gift-giving, there are motives of espionage on our ogorod (vegetable garden). A look at how far along another is with their planting, admire, make mental notes on whether their lines of seeds are straight, if their weeds are showing. The smirk on his face tells me we are behind, we pose no threat. My grandmother remarks that the neighbour has more help. Tonight it rained.

Holidaying on the sea, swimming all day, I fall asleep still feeling I'm floating in the waves. Here, when I shut my eyes, I see the fertile soil, dark brown like wet coffee grains, I see the rhythm of turning it over, digging it up only to place it back over the kartoshka (potatoes) and fertiliser, two-year-old cow manure I bury. A slow tide in the land.

I sit outside the living room on a Soviet-designed sofa bed. Covered in blankets and pleds (thick wool blankets). My stomach is full of warm memories of lunch: food from the soil, food grown here. Small potatoes and carrots left from last year's harvest could be used for planting, boiled on their own. They taste full of soil they have grown in. I remember eating them when I was young, in summer when it was warm. Family lunches with my aunt and uncle, I was always allowed the tiniest potato, the baby, the sweetest one of the batch, a pain to peel.

'Can you believe your grandma's making soup out of nettles?' I remember my uncle Serozha say. Now, fifteen years later, the nettles sting my hands as I chop them for my own soup. In your attempts to cook it feels fair that your food bites back a little. Taste the earth it has grown in. To eat with potatoes and carrots, washed outside and put out to dry on the grass.

My uncle Seryozha died quite young, he bought the Dacha ready to create a working haven. His death brought an unexpected halt to proceedings. Most of the house has signs of great plans, never to be realised. Mattresses, no bed, no inside toilet, no plumbing, hob but no gas source. The outside soon followed the disarray. Now, my aunt avoids the location, perhaps for fear of happy memories of the past, of Seryozha. Memories that remain here may become soiled if returned to in the present. Her visits dwindled more and more as the years passed. The only frequent visitor is Babushka, remaining true to the garden. Fearless of the overwhelming and ever-growing jobs. If anything, the relentless cleaning, planting, cutting and storing only power her on. Disregarding anyone else, I hear her tinkering, cleaning, chopping, loading.

It's cold, uncharacteristically so compared to my memories of this place in the heat of the summer in my childhood. We sleep with hot water bottles as our only source of warmth, aside from the small space heater that pumps dusty hot air into the room, and occasionally gives tantrums, cutting out in protest, exhausted by this place, a constant resident.

Fields surround the village.

Field at the Dacha.

I don't want to leave,
It's cold here
I don't want to go home,
There's no running water

The work is hard but good.
Our nails are dirty.

We brush our teeth with rainwater. The only music that I can access without internet is an old breakup playlist: my grandma dances to Rihanna.

I trim berry bushes. The blackberries fight back with thorns. I try to explain to them why the dead branches must fall, the way it must be for the bush to bear fruit in future. I find myself thinking in Russian, something people always ask about but to which I have usually no concrete answer. Here there is no English speaking, just reading, writing, my thoughts in Surzhyk now.

When I look outside the window these trees trick me into thinking it's colder than it is, it's snowing for a second as blossom falls.

Tricky cherry trees to pick, my Babushka tells me, the branches have grown too high. Babushka consoles me: 'it feeds the birds and what would you do with more than a bucket anyway?'

Here, my pen seems to glide as I write, maybe today it feels quick, hands used to pushing the Soviet mower.

I try not to be too precise, admiring the imperfect trimmings. I watch out for sticks and rocks, gathering before I mow, mainly apricot pips from the trees that line the path from the grate, the trees Babushka proudly tells me she planted. These apricots no longer produce the fruit I remember from years before, the pips must be

Drawing of fruit in the fridge at the dacha.

from their past. I remember eating these apricots when I was a child, too many to be desirable. Overripe or broken apricots, not flawless like their supermarket cousins, things I only now appreciate.

When there was more than we could eat (there always was), Babushka and Tetya Zhana would make jam, the sweet smell of fruit. The kitchen is constantly packed with kilos of sugar. Sugar, ever-present in the kitchen for the jam-making days. Eaten still warm with pancakes was the best. But no filling rivalled the forbidden condensed milk. Forbidden by my Mama, the viscous sugar entered our bloodstream with the traitorous aid of Babushka – my mother's injunction only making it imperative to eat too much in one sitting. Load it in with sticky hands, the innocent and worthy apricot jam left to stand on the table untouched and forgotten.

A moth flies and settles, yellow walls and fingernails of dirt. I lie in bed, a light, the moth homes in on the man-made sun. It has flown to its dying place unknowingly. It will probably never emerge into real sun again. Dogs bark, cricket so loud, projected through yellow walls. New windows, as we clear a patch of weeds, we say 'we have made a window to Europe', a joke in the context of civil war.

That night a storm, thunder and lightning, I was too tired to truly appreciate – I wish I could have been awake to watch the apple tree break. I wake to find Babushka outside in the storm picking apricots. I fall back asleep to the smell of jam.

A different kind of storm

After a year in Ukraine, I return to England with a newfound home in my motherland. This love dominates my work, something I can't quit. I explain the history, the unfairness of it all, the beauty in its new independence.

Map of the Golden Gate area: home is bottom left.

I find I miss Kyiv, the energy, the golden light of the sun as the jazz band plays, serenading me home as I walk from the metro rather than the tube – a memory, a dream. In England it's headphones blasting Primal Scream on the wet walk from Surbiton station, I'm walking to my badly insulated student house. I miss my newfound and now deserted home.

I make plans for return, to live, to work there.

And then we start hearing reports on the news.

At first, we joke, 'oh yeah, he was meant to invade today.' 'What day is he invading again?'. I worry, but we don't take it seriously, I joke with my dad about it on the phone. This week they are in England. My brother's school is on Easter holidays, usually, he would go to Kyiv for the holidays. By chance this time they have come to England instead.

30 days

On the 24th of February around 3.00 am UK time, Putin invades Ukraine, the war begins – oh no sorry,* sorry, my mistake … 'the Special Military Mission' begins. Call it what you wish, but wake me from this nightmare.

I message Alice – to an unusually quick response. The light-hearted nature, the normality of the way we write calms me. In disbelief we joke. I message Nikita next, who is nineteen – he tells me he is in a bomb shelter in the metro.

Messages to Nikita.

On the third day of Putin's invasion I make borsch and think of Babushka, and check for replacing 'grandma', 'grandmother' for 'Babushka', (getting consistency will avoid distractions). So far, I haven't said anything on social media, anything feels wrong to post. But today, I post to Instagram:

They say we are on the edge 'kraina'.
The edge of war, the border of freedom, the lip of truth,
the rim of a samogon bottle home-brewed with unknown
percentage, Putin drunk on power
Political edging on peace, sexual frustration hangover
from no love, no sex in the USSR.

The same men with different faces in power again, again.
Oligarchs camouflaged in orange protest scarves.
For salo over truth in the back of a Kamaz truck.
Our fields of grain, the breadbasket
In the heat of fire, our people rise, no need for yeast

I dream of bossy Babushki, dancing to new wave techno,
in metros used as bomb shelters with an energy induced by

spent years waiting in blood and cheap aeroplane tickets.
Unfashionable men drink alcohol free kvas, brewed from
the fermented wheat in the yellow of our flag.

Putin? My little swallow under your hunting boot, I can
hear you on the radio.
Stop telling people about this torn place,
NATO whispers 'please don't' promises and pledges
revolution ongoing

Hear mill plates grinding, sounds like the tanks
indefinitely pursuing propaganda on the edges
I can smell bread baking
Ghosts of red dabbed onto one's fist like smetana
Buttoning your coat, you notice your sickle is gone, left in
the fields with the wheat decomposing
There is no bread as you get to the end of the queue

You can't salt your kasha with gold if Putin has your
harvest
Money on the fields does not grow, before golod – famine.
Holodomor

Death by Stalin
Death by Putin

Oh hey helpful texters who after Radio 4
Message to ask me what they can do, they are so eager to
help me
How?
Maybe you can tell me how to cry

I don't know how to cry, I don't know how to cry for the
past mass hunger
the loss of the mother tongue my mother doesn't speak,
Babushka's pension
The fire, the blood, the future.

I don't know how to cry in Ukrainian,
for unanswered lies
useful pain
Unheard words, unanswered prayers, I can smell the
beeswax candles lit in St Sophia as bodies without limbs
arrived torn

Whispering, now muttering
When ordering a coffee in Ukrainian becomes a political
statement
The 'w' on a flat white becomes a v, boodlaska (please)
All I want is independence served with brunch on
Reitarskaya
As long as it is shown on an Instagram infographic

Again and again, so much for breaking through to Evropa
The child of a quiet Ukrainian mother, interrupted by
laws dictating voice
She is tough and hard and proud

Putin beats her into a sickle,
But she does not fracture, her spirit embedded,
strengthened with every blow
Mother this land, great to taste deep gold of our grain.
Independence teetering on changing borders.

You will feel in the price of bread the voice on the radio said
I will feel it on my chest

I hope your family is ok
Reoccurring reassuring
Effacing all feeling and meaning
But Ukraine is not dead yet, put away your shrine
Slava heroyam. Heroyam slava

I remember the street and I remember
complaining about the hill
I remember the view as I looked from the roof,

BOMBS
When I shut my eyes
Again. And again. And again
Babushka is tired, my motherland too.

This, my first activity on social media aside from the continuous stream of messages I read on Telegram from Ukrainska Pravda, updating me on the recent atrocities that keep me up.

Around only English people, the reality of the situation hasn't hit me. He invaded on Thursday. In a daze, except for when I hear the occasional updates on my radio, I continue with life as usual.

THE TIMES
SCOTLAND

On the front line
Battle to save Kyiv

i

Putin bombs civilians

Batman's brilliant return

Daily Mail

UKRAINE REFUGEE APPEAL

Now you send our fund soaring past £2million

PRAY FOR KYIV

PM warns Putin is bent on reducing capital to rubble ++ 40-mile column of tanks poised to strike ++ Rockets rain down on second city Kharkiv

Mirror

The Heart of Britain   We stand by Ukraine

A boy is born in a bomb shelter beneath Putin's murderous assault on Kyiv

For his sake... for his future... STOP

THE TIMES

Putin lays waste to cities

Russian captives cry for their mothers

THE TIMES

A dark day for Europe

The thumps grew louder. War was here

On Friday I go out with my friends, then we decide to have people round for afters. I don't care about the mess. I hear people whispering about me. Every time I close my eyes, dancing, I see flashes of bombs, but I decide to ignore them. F keeps trying to kiss me, I feel like a prude because I don't touch him, I can't. I feel numb, my arms heavy, any movement feels awkward and forced. How can I respond to 'are you OK?'

Phil (my dad).

Lada (Mama).

The next morning I wake up early and tired. I'm going down to Somerset to meet my family. I'm looking forward to it, but I fuck up the trains and it takes me five hours rather than the usual three. They pick me up from the station and the war is all they talk about in the car. It's overwhelming, it's all they talk about. I still feel sick from the night before, but they just go on and on, making predictions, like gamblers betting on things they can't control.

We go to my dad's favourite pub, he calls it 'dog pub' because of all the dog walkers. I look at my parents and feel angry; it's just so unfair.

They both came from so little, they built so much. My childhood, they spent at work. Working towards some light, some balance, some wealth which they finally found in the last few years. They paid off their debts, and for the first time in my recollection there was no constant fear. They deserved their newfound pleasures. They had worked fucking hard and what looked to be a comfortable retirement has been put in jeopardy. 'It's certainly not lost yet, so far we're OK, not as comfortable as we were, but OK – so far...' Phil comments.

The next day after lunch, Beatty calls Babushka, the phone on speaker. I laugh when she says the canary got loose and the cat almost ate it, she had to throw stuffed toys at it to try to get it down.

She tells me my cousin's lifelong depression is cured,... 'he just needed the war and good sex'. He's a new man, she jokes.

She comments she can hear bombs, the sirens will start up soon. 'Babushka idi v niz' idi v niz' (go downstairs), my brother Alfie says, encouraging Babushka to go down to hide in the bunker. Babushka delays going downstairs because she wants to finish telling me about her latest racy novel.

I don't know when I'll next see her.

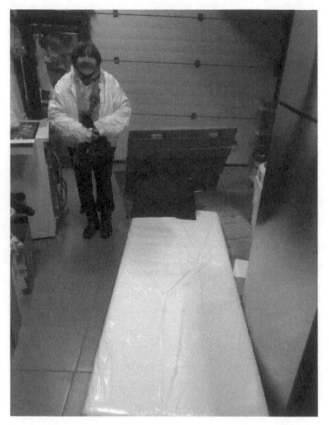

Babushka in bomb shelter, set up in basement of our apartment building.

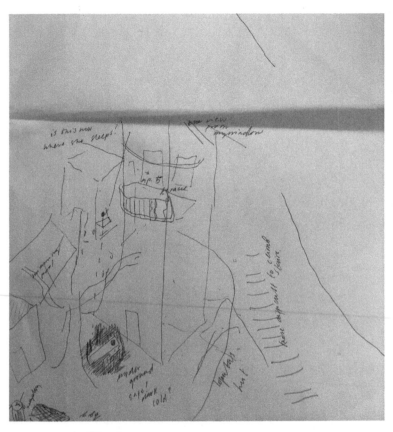

Mapping our building from memory.

My sister Beatty is twenty, the only one who comes close to Babushka as the best person I know. I don't want her to go back to Glasgow where she studies, instead asking her to come back to London with me.

The next two weeks in London are a blur of protests in the rain, baking, collecting clothes and art for weekly sales. It is exhausting. Beatty stays with me in my bed, we watch *Servant to the People* every night, Ukrainian President Zelenskiy's comedy TV show before he became an unlikely politician and then President.

The protests are badly organised, these people are running on no sleep, they are shouting in horse voices. Their main speaker, a girl my age, shouts slogans: 'SLAVA UKRAINI!' 'SLAVA HEROYAM!' we shout back, for two hours this is a rallying cry that keeps us going as our legs tire from standing. I enjoy the Ukrainian music they play, Ukrainian Eurotrash, the sort of songs usually heard in a taxi in Kyiv, they now make me cry with pride. Each day I pick up more and more lyrics to sing along. They save the anthem for last, which starts with the line 'Sche ne vmerla Ukraina', which translates to 'Ukraine has not died yet', how awfully fitting.

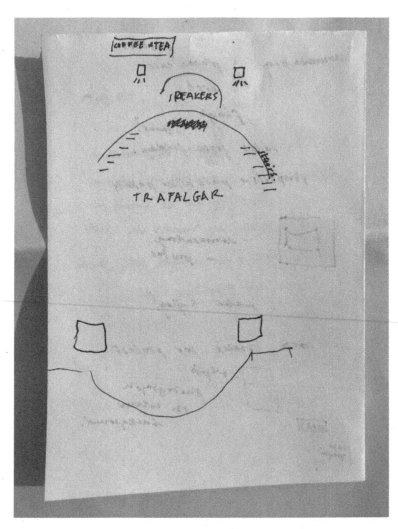

Map of protests.

HUNGRY?

BUY CAKE

TODAY IN KP
RECEPTION

ALL PROFITS TO
UKRAINE

HELP SAVE MY
BABUSHKA!

You bake

I sell

all profits to UKRAINE

We help UKRAINE
BRING baked goods
BUY baked goods
Thusday 11th
12th

KINGSTON BORSCH
TAKE-AWAY CLUB

I make Borsch
You eat Borsch

We help UKRAINE

all profits to UKRAINE

FUNDRAISING

UNTIL

THE WAR ENDS !

Could you be the lucky
winner of gift basket
worth over £100?

Bottle of Prosecco
Scented candle
Chocolate
Signed print
Set of postcards
+ Mystery Gift
... and more

only
£2!

Raffle for Ukraine!

YOU CLEAN
WARDROBE

I SELL CLOTHES

YOU BUY CLOTHES

WHEN: Monday 7th and Monday
14th March.
WHERE to drop/buy: KP
RECEPTION

67

By the end of the first week my memories of singing it every day at school come back as I can recite the whole thing, loudly bellowing along with fellow Ukrainians in the square.

The unfairness of it all strikes me. That week, I spitefully look at my friends in the library. I wish you had a war. I think I wish they all did.

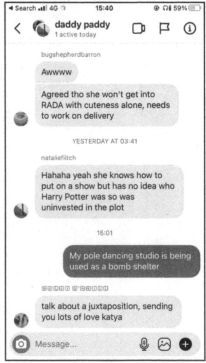

Messages to Alice.

They help with baking and selling their clothes and artwork. They come to marches yet I feel I feel angry, they don't do enough I think, only projecting the feeling I have that I am not and will never do enough.

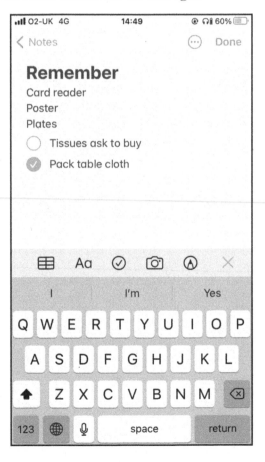

On day five, while Beatty and I sit in the library, we plan for our next sale, printing posters, buying napkins, asking for clothes. I write about last night's bombings on Babi Yar, a Jewish memorial site from WW2;

Babi Yar WW2.

Babi Yar 2022.

I'm in shock,
They said never again, again and again for 80 years.

We grow up looking in horror at history books
It was easy then, questioning how they turned a blind eye,
how they chose not to see.

How it was easier to keep going, prioritise your life, have
a nice time.
I'm sorry I don't mean to tell you off.

A bomb drops on Babi Yar, the largest killing site of Jews
in WW2.
Five more bodies to add to the count.
Combustible remembrance it seems.

If you stay deaf, history repeats itself louder.

Don't smile at me and ask if I'm OK. We are strong but we
are dying.
Send arms, close the sky.

It's snowing in Kyiv, and they fight
It's cold in the metro where they sleep,
Where you hope it's the signal when they don't pick up.

This is not our war, it's his killing site.
Don't make Ukraine a memorial.

After lunch I argue with a friend, L.

L: Can I use a table to sell tickets for my event? Are you using them all, I can go on the side
K: No, I'm using them
L: Have you even booked them all?
K: L, people are dying, you can't have a table

Later he apologises

It felt like it wasn't real, it's not mine. It's a film I'm watching. On day six I write:

I'm angry
I miss having fun

I miss my friends though they are here to support me
I miss being able to think
I hate that I'm jealous of those without war
I feel guilty my war has ruined their pancake plans

I think of Babushka, when will her water be cut by Putin —
the gas? How long will her food last, the families, children
cold in the metro
How long will this last, no marker on this hard time
I message another friend, I wake up making irrational
promises, prayers
I see a bomb is dropped in Kyiv, but I don't know where,
who has been hit
My mind is kasha

I feel proud of my people, united as ever, more than ever

I see our strength
I hear our language, the beauty of which is not expressed
in translation
I feel our anger
Our humour, our practicality
His military size is unparalleled in our strength of spirit

Passers-by, friends, strangers stop to chat as I sit and sell at the table,

A: You've been here ages man, fuck me these cakes are expensive
K: It's for Ukraine
A: Shit man
K: I want to buy a tank, I found one on ebay

On the seventh day Babushka calls again. This time I answer.

'It's cold, it's snowing outside, I gave him your father's gloves – I hope he doesn't mind', she speaks quickly. I can't get a word in edgeways.

She continues, 'I went through our biscuit cupboard, I found all the chocolate we have from Christmas to give to those hiding in the metro.'

I respond, 'Have you been writing?' She previously mentioned she had brought paper and pens to record this time. In response, her voice breaks, 'Every time I sit down to write I cry, what is there to write about now?'

I message Nikita to check if he is OK – I ask him if he has heard from Alice.

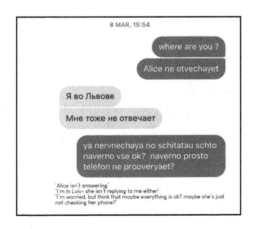

Week 2

On day eight I feel tired of repetitive conversations, everyone on tenterhooks around me. I haven't had much sleep. I think selfish thoughts of the holidays I had planned for Kyiv this summer. I'm in a toxic cycle of sleeping with my phone in my room.

HEAR OUR SPIRIT
OUR VOICES WILL BE HOARSE
Bombs on the metro stop called 'Friendship of the People"
She was happier today
The woman on the street still sells flowers
We see a man with a Marlboro cigarette in his mouth
dispose of a bomb on TikTok
Russian soldiers missing mama
Old women handing out sunflower seeds
'May something good come of you when you die"
Zelenskiy tired, his eyes wide
I'm angrier
What if I never see my street again

On day ten I call my dad and he repeats 'we can't be victims' again and again. He sounds like he is trying to convince himself. That evening I write:

We are not dead yet
I'm strong but I feel so weak
I don't have tears to cry
My cough won't stop
I don't care or have time anymore
A great time to stop seeing someone
He says he is having a difficult time

Everytime Babushka calls, I am scared it is the last time, that I will hear the bomb that kills her. That day I write in the morning:

You grow up
Things get harder, darker
Your plans for pancake day fall mute as war goes on
You think of Babushka
How she would make pancakes in stacks, with jam she
would make from apricots fallen from her tree at the Dacha

You have a cold and your cough continues,
An attack on your body as Putin attacks your home, your
people and the places you love
I feel so alone
Will it ever end
I feel so tired, nothing I will do feels enough
I can't save it
I don't know

You will feel it in the price of bread
I will feel it in my chest.
In my heart
In Babushka's voice as it shakes on the phone
In our golden fields

When Babushka doesn't pick up I know at least she's safe underground. After years of trying to teach her, it takes a war for her to learn how to use Facebook. That's where she checks the news she tells me. She insists I listen to her new favourite Slovakian singer she has discovered on 'The Youtube'.

I overthink calling her. I put it off. When we speak she talks and I can hear her thoughts are kasha (the Ukrainian word for porridge). In the moments she talks at length barely taking a breath, I think about all the work I would be doing while we speak. I then feel guilty that I am not really listening. Looking back, maybe the frustration I feel is because I so viscerally feel her scrambled state, frustrated because it so acutely reflects my own. She goes on in a continuous flow of small insignificant things like what she had for lunch. Her commentary is peppered with deep sighs and outcries over the horrible amounts of life wasted in this war.

On day seventeen a friend sends me an article that describes how Sainsbury's has changed the name of their 'Chicken Kiev' to the Ukrainian spelling, 'Chicken Kyiv'. Small victories cheer me up.

Sainsbury's renames chicken kievs and pulls Russian-made vodka

UK's second biggest supermarket switches Soviet-era spelling of capital city to preferred Ukrainian version

○ **Russia-Ukraine war: live news**

📷 Sainsbury's plans to change its chicken kyiv packaging in the coming weeks. Photograph: Graeme Robertson/The Guardian

Sainsbury's is changing the name of its chicken kiev to chicken kyiv and is joining Waitrose, Aldi and Morrisons in withdrawing a Russian-made vodka from the shelves in the latest action by British retailers to signal solidarity with the people of Ukraine.

The UK's second biggest supermarket said the packaging for the poultry dish would change in the next few weeks, switching the Soviet-era name for the country's capital for the Ukrainian version.

The move comes after several smaller operators announced a switch to chicken kyiv, including the Better Naked brand and Essex-based Our Local Butcher. Marks & Spencer, which popularised the dish in the UK after making chicken kiev one of the first ready meals in 1979, has also come under pressure to rename the dish.

Guardian article on Sainsbury pro Ukrainian Kyiv spelling.

I don't think he'll win
Hopeless predictions
Helpless hopes
Will the message read more death or ceasefire

On day eighteen I remember feeling so angry. On the news I see images of Ukrainian flesh burnt and split. In the headlines. I think about the horrible Kyiv cream cake that I've never tried, and now may never get to.

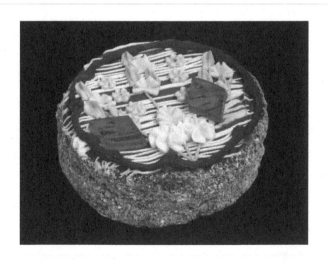

A butcher, a bandit
Machine gun loaded with his sausage fingers

A senseless pile of death
Trapped
Hungry cold, bloody faces turning green

His soldier's lamb chops, as if thrown to dogs on the floor
with no care
Young boys with no memories, no food only lies

Our people are the same; the Russian soldiers, just
numbers to count as they pile up,
Pregnant with hope, mother pregnant with child dies in
bombing.

Slabs fired on the barbecue
Cities sizzle
Greedy man wipes his greasy bile-stained sleeves on others,

Babushka left to clean up the mess, bloodstained trapki in
her strong knuckled hands with veins visible

She's seen death before, ever repeating misery unfairly enforced.

So little man, young in age, seeking glory, all you leave is bloodstains,
A sour taste of death

As we wait to clean, for fields to grow gold with wheat again, we wait for the smell of fresh-baked bread,

Until such a time the memory will sustain us, until we hold its crust in our hands once again.
Our flour no longer stained with red.

On the corner of the golden gate metro she gives out flowers,
The war will not move her

Don't question the strength of Ukraine, our unity

Do not forget

Flower seller.

Babushka who is making Molotov cocktails

Zhenya our engineer with red hair who cannot leave her disabled father so lies in the bath of their apartment building when the air raid sounds.

Pasha an IT man who fixed my laptop is now fighting on the front.

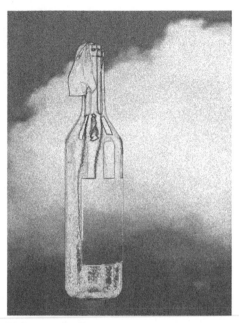

Molotov cocktail.

The woman knocked a drone out of the sky with a jar of pickles.

The woman who handed sunflower seeds to armed Russian soldiers saying
'May something good come of you when you die''

The stopping of tanks by unarmed civilians

You question the strength of Ukrainian spirit?

They will last 2 days, then 6, maybe 2 weeks.

They will last...

We will last
She ne vmerla ukraina
We are not dead yet
They will keep going, the war will end

On the phone my grandma's voice sounds tired as we speak of when this will all end.

'...so much to fix, there will be so much...' Her voice breaks.

'we will, but that's OK, cleaning... we know how to do that.'

I rarely feel aggression, that's not how my anger usually feels.

University newsletter
'*The River*' article.

On day nineteen I'm interviewed by someone from the
Kingston *River* newspaper. His article is badly written,
accurate to my words but reads like a GCSE mock exam.

I wanted them to call a cease-fire
I wanted them to leave

I hate hearing of humanitarian aid
Why can't you just leave

I can hear children playing
And screaming,
Like they should be in the school next door
Joyful screams
Unlike the ones I imagine 12 km from the border of Poland

I keep getting distracted when I cook, little burns on my hands, the injuries look pathetic compared to the faces of Ukrainians burnt and plastered over the headlines.

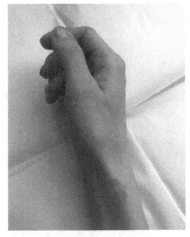

Burn on my wrist.

The next day I hear on the radio

'You know it's not the first time Russia has used hunger against Ukraine... in 1932...' I hear a podcast on Radio 4. They are talking about the situation in Mariupol, people dying of cold, hunger and lack of water. A modern Holodomor, while memories of the Lenin induced famine linger. The notion of any famine in Ukraine is ironic and laughably unfair. Often referred to as the breadbasket of Europe, it is home to its incredibly fertile soil called chernozer or black earth.

I find a photo of me doing ballet from the same era. A stark contrast to the little girl I saw on Instagram today whose leg has been blown off by Russian missiles.

On day twenty-one I'm running a raffle; I sit again at a table trying to raise money, the minute scale of which makes me feel pathetic. Today I'm running the stall alone. I suddenly am so conscious of how far behind I am, my friends always going off to do work. I feel bitter. I try to be positive to the few who buy a ticket. Some laugh and I cheer up a bit. Tempting people:

Would you like to enter the raffle? I ask again and again, sometimes successfully interesting a passer-by.

One woman responds

'No, I'm not feeling lucky'.

'Oh but the prize is worth over a hundred pounds', I say with a smile, 'you never know, it could be your lucky day, and if you don't – all profits go to Ukraine', I respond light-heartedly, 'it's a win-win really'.

'I've already donated to Ukraine, so I'm not going to be made to feel guilty,' she snaps in retort. That day I write:

Now I feel guilty
It only took a week for everyone to get bored
Stop caring, move on with life

They'll be sick of me
They are sick of me

The next day I run a bake sale and the same woman comes past. Her friend buys something, I feel awkward. I apologise and explain how close this is to my heart, knowing full well I am not in the wrong, I still feel guilty, insecure at what I've been pushing. She highlighted how needy I have felt of late, how much of my happiness, my self-worth, has depended on people's donations, dictated by their reactions. She accepts my apology and says she doesn't trust student bake sales for fear of them being unhygienic. This woman is horrible. She tells me she will make an exception this time and asks which one of the cakes is the cleanest. She buys five for a pound each.

A girl from Ukraine has been baking for me. She makes huge piles of big apple-filled buns. Larger than my fist, and rock solid, they do not look particularly appealing.

Nobody buys them, even when the price is dropped to 50p. I give them away for free, not knowing how to tell her as it happens over three weeks.

'Listen, I've baked, now they will cool down a little and I will bring, but I just don't know, which container to bring.'

I check my Viber messaging app for the first time in weeks. I only use it in Ukraine, the last messages are to the group I did yoga with every Monday and Wednesday last year. I am surprised to see it has been active in the last month.

Chat titled: Yoga 13:00, Wednesday, Friday. Tatjana Zolotar: 'Svetochka, hold on! We will have many more yoga lessons.'

I read a stream of messages, someone has shared a news article.

Svetlana (yoga teacher) was evacuating Kyiv with her family, they were a car of four civilians. *Attacked by Russian fire,*
> *she has been shot,*
> *and now three of her family are dead.*

All the yoga ladies message concerns. Svetlana replies from hospital 'I am out of ICU, I am OK!'

Wed 2 Mar, 11:17

Are you ok ?

Are you drinking enough tea

Are you still in the woods

Are you with your brother?

Thu 3 Mar, 11:29

I love you I'm thinking of you

Sun 6 Mar, 16:41

Where are you

What are you thinking

Mon 7 Mar, 11:15

I love you

Today 12:07

I love you I hope you are ok

Delivered

On day twenty-one I message Alice again, for what feels like the hundredth time with no response.

My dad texts me a photo of a bullet found in our family car. The old Passat we joke will never die, with a history of breaking down over its twenty-one years has now been under fire.

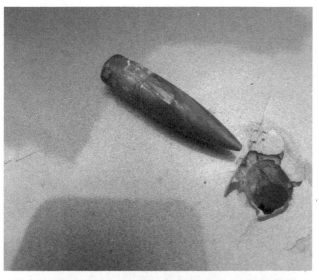

10 cm bullet found in family car.

At a party, 'You are so brave' says a face I don't know as they hold my hand and tell me they don't know what to say. I have half an hour to forget until the next conversation comes up.

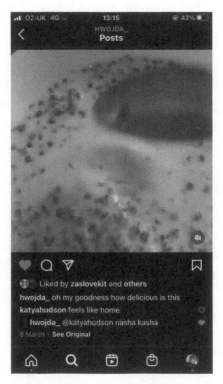

Sasha posts video of grechka on Instagram.

A confusion of handshakes and I don't know what to say, as if I am a widow before my time. Save your pity, stop talking about my motherland like it's dead, I'd rather you just buy me a drink.
Gory imagery has seeped into my subconscious, I dreamed I was hiding from bombs at the Dacha.

I message Theo, a family friend still in Kyiv; his dad, a Ukrainian writer, has been interviewed by Radio 4 again.

Bank transfer to Ukrainian Army.

On day twenty-five I've been putting off calling Babushka, I am conscious of it. Every time Beatty calls me she tells me it's important to talk to Babushka. But I am scared to call, I don't want to but I know I should.

Wake up every two hours to check the news
Live in a dream where driving a car would solve everything
This was my home

This was where we would drink coffee,
Don't waste my beautiful street
Superficial reasons I am angry for
I cry for death and destruction
This is my home
We will rebuild
A waste, a horrible waste. I try to transfer the money I
have raised money but the banks are down.
Compliments from strangers' satisfaction
so small
pat on the back as I can't send it for another day

Google Maps view of Golden Gate area. Family home is Ivana Franka St. 4.

On day twenty-seven I call Babuskka, record and transcribe it.

220322_0064.wav

List of acronyms: K=Katya Hudson Z=Zhanna Babushka)

begin transcript 00:00:00]

Z: Zelenskiy is speaking and is speaking in
English,
Of course I don't really understands you all of
course are more equipped in English and of course
it it better when it is explained in Ukrainian,
but he's very proud of his country, his nation,
his people, says before Americans would lift
their passports and say I am a citizen of
America, USA
But he says now we, but we, maybe don't lift,
because he says , well of course I don't really
understand, you of course are more…eem

K: ahgaa...

Z: Well passport in part, but I also am very
proud

K: I also feel proud

Z: That you and Beatty have a connection to
Ukraine, very close

K: Yes of course

Z: I really feel that

K: Babushka

Z: Im very proud also...

K: Babushka! Today I sent 5500 to the Ukrainian
army

Z: what a good girl you are Katechka you are
such a good girl

Thank you,

Z: I love you, without this...

K: Well of course,

Z: But i'm just proud that you, people, you live
our worries, our distress, our suffering, our
losses , see, that you genuinely feel and try in
in some way, at least in some way, and this is
not just some way, this is very meaningful for
our peoples army, a big thank you
K: Don't say thank you

Z: Im proud, I don't even know how to reward you

K: Hug me babushka
*laughing
That will be the best reward

Z: How are you, tell me please

K: Im good I am taking a break from the
fundraising, I want to finish my project, its
about Ukraine, everything really

Z: Good girl good girl

K: So don't think that we are forgetting about
you, I think everything will be ok,

Z: Im very proud of you al, I'm so glad, so
happy that I have you

[explosion heard in distance 03.42]

Z: There, how strongly we can feel the explosion

K: Yes?

Z: Mhmm, it seems very close..

K: So maybe you go downstairs?

Silence…

Z: …well ill see, it it was something Sasha
would have called me or come up..

… He yesterday spent all day driving to get his
car
A do you know there are some lowlife people,
Ukrainians but you can feel that they are not
Ukrainians, you can see that they hate this
country because they try in anyway to help, you
understand its not for nothing they say that
Russians found airport targets through traitors
all thanks to them, they tell them where and how
our people are so good,, independent, but also
foreigners who heard of the conflict came, not
long ago-
They say they understand what war is and danger
is, but want to help Ukraine, to help support

Katechka, sunshine,

K: Yes?

Whats the weather like?

K: This week its been really warm, I'm sitting outside

Z: Listen, we have a curfew, so because of these low-lives we cant go outside,

K: You cant go outside at all?

Z: Because of these defectors, they will try to find them and destroy them

[bomb heard in distance 05.42]

K: Babushka idi v niz (go downstairs)

Z: Horrible -

K: Go down I'm worried

Z: Maybe actually,

K: Yes go downstairs

Z: Ok Katechka I'm going downstairs so ok good thank you for calling me

K: I love you babushka

Z: So if you can call me at least once a week, its very nice for me and you can tell me about your work

```
K:   Go, yes, listen, call me too

Z:   Hhhmm, I'm going

Ok bye
Thank you for everything I love you and kiss you
five though sand million times.

K:   I love you too

Z:   I love you so much, ok

K:   Ok Babushka, ok


[End transcript 00:06:25]
```

On day twenty-nine, I write:
I listen to videos of sirens
I cry, I swallow

On day thirty, I write:
It's been 30 days since Putin invaded

And now

How long will this journalling last? I start to realise how long this will go on. When can I stop writing? I realise it needs to end somewhere, the thought of this never-ending war fills me with dread. I decided to cut it off at thirty days.

Life teeters between the daily mundane and extremes. Normality occasionally, as I go out with friends. Whenever a drunk stranger introduces themselves I have a different reaction when they ask where I am from. People still come up to me at uni and tell me it's an amazing thing I did. In looped conversations, when people are stuck on what to say and to be fair there isn't any good answer. Nothing that they can say will help.

Sometimes I want to talk about it, sometimes I don't. Sometimes this great expectation of needing to be a mouthpiece for all of Ukraine. Sometimes I feel like a dark burden on company, sometimes I make jokes that people are scared to laugh at.

Two weeks ago in a trough of particularly low self-worth, I started seeing F again. It was nice to feel liked again, I knew it wouldn't last. Again, I felt I had other more pressing things on my mind.

My parents come to stay in London, cat-sitting for English family friends who use to live in Kyiv, with whose daughter I use to do ballet lessons. She tells me her work is tiring, doing something financial I don't understand. When will this war be over? Endless conversations over the dinner about the future, the same utterances on repeat.

Mama spends days cleaning and making connections between English people offering their homes and Ukrainians she knows who want to get out of Kyiv. The architect who worked in their office and her twin six-year-old daughters will be in a small village in Somerset soon. Yulia, a lady who was a cleaner in Kyiv is keen to come. She can't speak English. Mama worries she won't fit in in Hastings.

For the last few weeks, my mum has been mentioning that she might go back to Kyiv to get Babushka. She cannot drive, so the lack of possibility means I give it little thought. She applies for a visa for Babushka, hoping she may live with some family. Later, Mama tells me her plans are cementing, she wants to fly to Poland and then get the train from there. She wants to go home, she says she feels like a foreigner here.

Mama has called me and told me she is going to Kyiv to get Babushka. I think this is a good idea, she needs some company and I want to hug her.

I print my book for hand in, first I fuck up the printing, now the cutting.

The binding is all wrong and ugly and I feel useless. I compare myself to other people. I feel utterly unemployable and undesirable. I worry about the future, I think about money.

My silly little book feels insignificant, I realise I need to start again. I again have a moment of retrospection, on the chaotic nature of life in the last few months. Deadlines carry varying levels of significance depending on the day.

Mama calls me and says she is going to Kyiv on Tuesday. She has booked her flight. She says she will stay a month, this is news. She says she won't leave with Babushka. I'm scared, I don't want her to stay there. I keep thinking about how she might die.

Tomorrow she will go.

All-day when people ask how I am I tell them. Getting confused between the boundaries for friends and strangers. How are you? I reply that my mum is going to Kyiv and it's a bad idea. 'My mum has decided to go back to Kyiv, I think it's a bit stupid.' A snippet in passing conversation I quickly move on from as nobody knows how to respond.

I talk to my tutor about how I am unhappy with my project. I want an extension to finish writing this book. A friend helped me apply for mitigating circumstances a few months ago. As evidence, we just uploaded a *Guardian* front-page article that reads 'Putin invades Ukraine'.

That evening I get offered a job on a set.

I am working so I only manage to sporadically message Mama once or twice. I haven't heard from her yet but I hope she calls when she gets to Kyiv.

As I sit down to write. Babushka calls me. I am confused because she hasn't mentioned Mama and I am scared to ask.

Babushka says she needs to get money for Mama. She's being driven from Ternopil and her phone is dying – the last thing I heard she was going to take the bus – my dad said this was safer than trains as Putin is known to bomb them. It all feels so real but also intangible. I feel like I might cry sitting in the library, at her bravery, out of fear.

My mum calls me from Kyiv. She says she ordered sushi for dinner on her first night. She went out and got a haircut. Yesterday, she took my grandma out to dinner, tomorrow she will go to the veg market to make dinner for some friends coming round.

Pasha, an IT man she works with who I mentioned earlier, is fighting on the front – has been shot, but is alive. She tells me of the package of body wash, chocolate and kasha (porridge) she has sent him.

Grechka, kasha (porridge).

Mama tells me Babushka has run off to the Dacha to check on her cherry trees – there is fruit to collect.

Babushka June 2022.

She sends me videos of beautiful Ukrainians having clothes sales, food markets, drinking coffee on the weekend. They won't let Putin ruin their Spring, they will continue living. Today marks one hundred days since the war started and Sche ne vmerla Ukraina – Ukraine is not dead yet.

St Sophia Square (short walk from family home).

Ivana Franka St.

Postscript

I come from Ukraine; it's been a year since I've been home.

I know Alice is still alive from our sporadic messages.

My little brother Alfie tells me when he turns eighteen he wants to join the army.

My sister Beatty, who is now in her second year of uni, still does sales to raise money; she's spending too much of her student loan to bake countless cakes. She went to Kyiv this summer: I was angry and worried, I said she was stupid and selfish. I didn't want her to die. But she didn't, instead, she went to the Dacha with my grandma, she dug potatoes, picked fruit, and pickled veg. Her back hurt from the hard labour, she got sunburnt, got used to the sirens at that point ignored. She went back to Ukraine and I was jealous and guilty I didn't.

My mum and dad are worried, away from the home they built. If the pipes freeze this cold winter - it's meant to be cold - they will burst and cause havoc.

Over the year Mama has become a regular on the journey to and from Kyiv. It's an aeroplane to Warsaw, train with the blinds down from there.

Life continues in Kyiv, sirens ignored, a new kind of normal since the war.

But this hopeful daze didn't last for long. The city that seemed to be safer is now dark to save electricity. The home that we thought was secure because of its central location and proximity to embassies is again in danger with bombs falling on the bridge and university a short walk away. And now it's winter and it's cold, so cold.

Babushka on the train leaving Kyiv.

Last time my mum went to Ukraine she brought Babushka back. Finally convinced to spend Christmas with us. It's cold in Kyiv, they predict it will get to -30. Babushka brought me socks from Ukraine. She is bored, she is panicked. When I stay, we share a bed, we try to only talk in Ukrainian, gossiping about life since we've been apart. A language we have always known, we now force ourself to speak. We struggle to find words but these days speaking Russian hurts.

She tells me about the harvest at the Dacha this year. So many potatoes, huge beetroots. No family around to eat them. I can't help but wonder whether the huge crop this year has anything to do with radiation from whatever foul missiles Putin has been chucking haphazard over our border. She tells me about the mass of walnuts, which she spent days collecting and drying, laid down on newspaper covering the floors of the Dacha. She tells me she sold these nuts to men who travel around the village in a van, four sacks worth. She proudly adds all the nut money has been sent on to the army - I'm not sure how much four sacks of walnuts go for these days...

The other day when I was vacuuming she mistook the sound for a siren. I take her to the salsa night for Ukrainian refugees in the village. The sun shines as we go on a walk and she tells me about the new sexy book she's reading, something about horse racing. After we greet a passer-by walking their dog she breaks my heart when she says 'how lucky people are to be happy without war'. I know she feels guilty to have left and she wishes she was home.

Babushka in England.

As for me, I've left uni now. I've lived in Paris for a few months. I've been working for a magazine. I'm back in England for Christmas. Staying on sofas and sharing beds. I spend my time seeing family, catching up with friends, I even went on a date. There's an awkward silence after I say I'm from Ukraine. Pity isn't sexy. I go Christmas shopping for books and walk past Zelensky's new book, amongst others on Ukraine and the war. Sometimes I forget the war, sometimes I have moments where I get hot and overwhelmed. The future is unknown, unpredictable. I try to embrace the freedom of not having a home to go to. It's been pushing me to try harder, do more. Without warning I remember Ukraine, sometimes when I don't catch myself, I cry in public. And so, the war goes on, I keep on living, in some new distorted version of reality.

And Now...

When people ask how Christmas was, I say it was nice. Being Ukrainian has some benefits, people can be incredibly kind, charitable. It was a year since we were last together. We spent Christmas 2022 in Kent (a friend was away on holiday and offered us her empty family home - not quite refugees we joke we are émigrés, it sounds more chic and less tragic). I shared a room with Alfie, Beatty was with Babushka, Mama and Phil together. Babushka and I developed a taste for Amaretto.

Babushka and the Hudson grandchildren preparing
Christmas Dinner, 2022.

I remembered Christmas we would have in Kyiv, the usual friends, family we would see. I think we all did, taking turns to cheer the death of Putin, Slava Ukraini (glory to Ukraine), Slava Heroyam (glory to heroes), Smert Voroham (death to enemies) ... You get the idea.

I don't know what's next, how long this war will last, when I will next be home. But I do know I am incredibly proud and privileged to be Ukrainian, I hope the West sends more arms, and I pray for Russians to wake up and put a stop to this destruction.

Do Peremohi (until victory).